FIVE STEPS
TO POSITIVE
POLITICAL DIALOGUE

For Emilia

best wishes

Amy Uelmen

About the
5 Steps Series

The books in the 5 Steps Series are useful for anyone seeking bridge-building solutions to current issues. The 5 Steps series presents positive approaches for engaging with the problems that open up gaps and divisions in family, school, church, and society. Each volume presents five short chapters (or "steps") on a single topic. Each chapter includes a relevant "excerpt", "insights" from the author(s), and an "example" to consider. The "example" is a real-life story that illustrates how each step can be applied in daily life.

Topics include:

- Facing Suffering
- Living Christian Unity
- Effective Student Leadership
- Towards Great Parenting
- A Fulfilling Marriage

FIVE STEPS
TO POSITIVE
POLITICAL DIALOGUE

Insights and Examples

Amy Uelmen

New City Press
of the Focolare
Hyde Park, New York

Published in the United States by New City Press
202 Comforter Blvd., Hyde Park, NY 12538
www.newcitypress.com
©2014 Amelia Uelmen

Cover design by Leandro de Leon

Library of Congress Cataloging-in-Publication Data

Uelmen, Amy.
  5 steps to positive political dialogue / by Amy Uelmen.
      pages cm
  Summary: "Uelman offers insights that lead towards believing it is
possible to have a positive vision of politics. She suggests
communication
needs to be based on a loving attitude. We should discover the place of
compromise. In the end, we can build the *polis* with constructive
action"--
Provided by publisher.
  ISBN 978-1-56548-507-5 (alk. paper)
  1. Communication in politics--Moral and ethical aspects. 2.
Compromise
(Ethics) I. Title. II. Title: Five steps to positive political dialogue.
  JA85.U45 2014
  172'.1--dc23
                                    2014011814

Printed in the United States of America

Contents

Step *3*

Step *4*

Step *5*

Introduction

"SO WHAT SHOULD WE do?" My friends were almost in tears. It was the summer before a presidential election, and the emails were flying. People who had been very close friends, committed to supporting each other in their efforts to live the gospel, found themselves trapped in the polarization that was also ripping apart many other communities. Multiple questions and fears arose. Are my misguided friends being inadvertently duped into making sinful choices by political machines? Are my misguided friends being inadvertently duped by political rhetoric that sounds good, but in practice produces no social change? How can I convince them otherwise? If we can't convince each other, where is our country going? If we can't have these conversations in a spirit of love and unity, where are we going?

My friends had come to me with their questions because I am a lawyer, and they hoped that I might have some particular insight. At that point, I was not exactly sure what to think or how to move either. Their questions and our common commitment to try to understand and love each other across political differences prompted me to delve into the teachings of the Roman Catholic Church on the topics of voting and citizenship.

In the years that followed, I had many opportunities to explore the nature of political life and political choices with people from across the political spectrum. An especially enlightening point in the journey was a weekend workshop devoted to developing tools for dialogue about politics. As my own perspective continued to emerge, I published a series of articles in law journals and in Living City, the Focolare's monthly magazine of religion, culture and dialogue. Much of the material in this book is based on those works and modified to fit this book's format.

I wish to thank the friends who have courageously explored how their commitment to a gospel-based lifestyle of mutual love can be lived in political life, especially amid political disagreement. Our common efforts are a hopeful sign that the polarization dividing our communities, our churches, and our country as a whole can be bridged. It is a tiny seed just beginning to sprout, full of life and potential. I look forward to its continued growth.

Step 1

Believe
that a Positive Vision
of Politics is Possible

*P*OLITICS. THE WORD ALONE seems to evoke negativity, frustration and fatigue. Why didn't I get that promotion or job opportunity? Politics. Why can't our national, state or local government ever seem to get anything done? Politics. Being "political" or labeled a "politician" is often a code word for someone who uses manipulative or underhanded tactics to advance a partial or personal agenda.

How might this negative mentality towards politics be transformed? Just opening this book and moving beyond the first paragraph is a sign of hope. The desire to reflect on one's own perspective on politics is a step in the right direction.

The very origins of the term "politics" suggest a seed for positive change. The word originates in thinkers like Plato and Aristotle, who outlined their vision for the ideal *polis*, the city or community as a whole. Acknowledging how the broad dimensions of politics touch our everyday lives lets us recognize that whatever our task in society, we share in the responsibility for the life of the community as a whole. What may seem small gestures in our daily lives as citizens—following traffic rules, serving on a jury, informed voting, communicating ideas and concerns to elected representatives—are possibilities to add our own tile to the mosaic of a healthy body politic.

Connecting "politics" with hope for positive change may even spark the desire for deeper commitment to the community as a whole. Many thoughtful Christians have been and continue to be drawn to service in politics. Such commitment offers, as Focolare founder Chiara Lubich notes, "the possibility of loving our neighbor in a crescendo of charity: from interpersonal love to an ever greater love towards the *polis*."

In fact, those who work in politics are, in a certain sense, in a privileged position. Addressing a large gathering of mayors and civic officials, Lubich described politics as "the love of all loves, which gathers into the unity of a common design the resources of persons and groups and provides the means for each one to freely fulfill his or her own vocation"[1]

Certainly the task of renewing political life is challenging. Even those who make sincere efforts to forge a consensus on implementing concrete proposals for positive change face conflicts and misunderstandings. And any position of responsibility or influence, whether in government or in the private sector, brings with it the temptation to misuse one's power.

Yet in his 1988 Apostolic Exhortation, *Christifideles Laici*, John Paul II left no doubt that Christians must seek to imbue the political realm with gospel-based values. He describes public life as "for everyone and by everyone," noting: "...the common opinion that participating in politics is an absolute moral danger does not in the least justify either skepticism or an absence on the part of Christians in public life." On the contrary, those who in a spirit of service dedicate their work to the public good deserve praise and encouragement (#42).

The vision of politics as "the love of loves," can inspire each of us to a hopeful, constructive, positive vision of politics and political life.

Real-Life Story
The Village with a Caring Heart[2]

My adventure in politics began when I responded to a letter from the mayor of North Riverside, Illinois, seeking ideas for his new Committee of Neighborhood Services. A short time later I was asked to be the program's coordinator.

There was no blueprint for the task of organizing 72 block captains. I suggested that the main goal should be to try to make each block more like a family, where no one would feel alone. The Art of Loving proposed by Chiara Lubich struck me as a good basis for this effort. I adapted it into a four-point "Art of Caring": 1) Be first to reach out to others; 2) Reach out to everyone; 3) Care concretely; 4) Be one with joys and sorrows.

During block captain meetings, I would illustrate one of the points with my own experiences, quotations from well-known people, and other examples of people who live the Golden Rule. Soon some of the block captains also started sharing how they had lived one of the points.

For example, one captain explained how their block had handled the problem of a new resident whose barking dogs were bothering the neighbors. Instead of complaining to the police, the captain and neighbors tried to reach out to the dog owner, baking cookies for her and even helping her catch her dogs when they escaped from her yard. Only later did they approach her with their concerns about how the constant barking was disturbing a newborn baby on the block. They were able to resolve the problem without confrontation.

To be the "be first to reach out," block captains have prepared welcome bags for new residents, sometimes including homemade cookies and at Christmas time, small live decorated trees. One block captain decided to give one of these trees to a man who had just been admitted to a nursing home. When his wife brought him the tree from the mayor and the village, he could not believe he had been chosen for this gift.

To "reach out to everyone," the captains knock on everyone's door, even those who seem harder to reach. One couple had not attended the annual block party for three years running. When they were finally able to come, the neighbors gave them a round of applause.

To "care concretely," block captains distribute information packets prepared for specific groups, such as seniors and families. One captain discovered that an older couple had no working stove, and when the mayor heard this he bought a stove for them with his own money.

To "be one with joys and sorrows" means taking an interest in people, especially those who are suffering in some way. They send cards, bring food, listen to people's troubles, and communicate particular needs by email.

The network built by the Art of Caring now embraces the entire town. It is not hard to find a volunteer to drive someone to the doctor, or to pick up some groceries for the homebound.

The mayor and town trustees also put the Art of Caring into practice. The way the mayor welcomed a block captain from another political party demonstrated his readiness to go beyond partisan interests.

A quarterly village newsletter reports "Angel Stories" so that many can share in the growing sense of community. One angel visited sick people, bringing everyone a rose; another grew tomatoes and shared them with her neighbors. An 88-year-old angel cut down a little tree for a widow who feared it would break her gutters. The mayor's "Angel Award" and appreciation cards continue to encourage these efforts to help our neighbors by going the extra mile.

The Art of Caring has also extended to neighboring towns, as we try to "love the other town as our own."

The Art of Caring has transformed our town, helping to create a true sense of family. As people drive around our town, they tell us how great they feel. They have even invited relatives to move here. One resident expressed it well: "I am so lucky to live in a village with a caring heart."

Step 2

Practice Communication Skills Based on Love

"*A*BOVE ALL, MAINTAIN CONSTANT love for one another..." (1 Pt 4:8). What is it about political discussions that can lead us to press the pause button on this phrase? The second step explores how to communicate while trying to keep love front and center, regardless of the depth of political disagreement.

We struggle to let a spirit of love into our political discussions partly because we are still trying to understand how the current means of communication have changed the way we relate to each other. These means allow anyone who so chooses to participate in media-based political conversation. Internet web logs ("blogs") have broken down the boundaries of opinion journalism, previously controlled by professional "gatekeepers." Anyone with a link to the Internet can share a perspective freely and broadly. Because money and influence matter less in getting one's message out, previously excluded voices can and do contribute to the exchange of ideas. In many ways this development is positive.

But there are also downsides to the self-revelation that these new technologies allow. Being constantly hooked up via a keyboard might make us think that we are communicating, but what we actually say can often be superficial or banal. Conversations shaped by new media tend to take the shape of short and immediate reactive bursts rather than thoughtful responses, which take more time to compose and more length to explain. Internet, cable, and satellite technologies also make it easier to find and interact with perspectives that align closely with one's own. Frequently reinforcing our own views can create an "echo chamber," making it difficult to broaden our personal horizons to take in alternative perspectives. Interacting via these means of communication can make us feel not enriched, but more lonely and isolated.

We also wind up misunderstanding each other or disagreeing because we type or text as if we were conversing with someone face to face, but we cannot see the other's facial expressions or read the body language that would have helped us to grasp the effect of our words on another person. I would not have pressed "send" had I realized she was just not in the mood for that kind of humor. Smiley emoticons aside, hasty messages often do not convey the intended tone, or express the full range of human emotions.

How might love make a difference in our approach to communication? Many have found a helpful guide to communication practices in the practical points of "art of loving," as explained by Chiara Lubich. For me the most valuable way to keep love before me as I communicate has been to place the children's version of the art of loving, the "Cube of Love" right in front of my computer. The sides of the Cube read: I love everyone; I love my enemy; I love Jesus in the other; I am the first to love; I share the other's joy or hurt; and we love one another.

"I love Jesus in the other" reminds me that God is present in all of my conversation partners, including those for whom that email is destined, including those who are the topic of my message or blogging. "I love everyone" has at times become "including those who are not on-line"—reminding me to not get so caught up in the email or on-line world that I lose track of the people right next to me, perhaps in the same office, perhaps waiting for an in-person conversation in the hall, on the phone, or during a real lunch break away from the computer. The perspectives of the "everyone" in my immediate physical vicinity may differ from my chosen internet or blog world, or circle of Facebook friends. Conversations with these colleagues and friends can open horizons that I would not have otherwise noticed.

"I share the other's joy or pain" invites me, before I press "send," to take a breath and ask: how will this message or blog sound in the ears and heart of the other? Do I even understand enough about what my readers are living to be sensitive to how they will receive this message? Do I need to take the time to listen more, perhaps via other means of communication, before jumping in with my own message?

A few times—especially during political campaign seasons—I have found myself in the thick of an on-line misunderstanding or a heated exchange. "I love my enemy" has been a powerful reminder to give the other the benefit of the doubt and to interpret the message with a more generous read. I remember an exchange where "I'm the first to love" became "I'm the first to stop typing"—in order to pick up the phone to suggest to a friend that we find a time when we could finish the discussion in person. Just saying, "Let's stop" prompted both of us to take a moment for serious reflection. We asked ourselves, "How is it that we can become so nasty when we are typing?" When we met the following week, he walked into my office with a chocolate bar. Giving me a hug, he said: "This is a peace offering, I am sorry for being intemperate." I pulled out some homemade chocolate chip cookies, saying, "I am sorry, too." Looking each other in the eyes, our conversation took a completely different turn. We did not agree on everything, but our friendship has lasted far beyond that election season.

"We love one another" is a reminder that authentic relationships require multi-faceted work. While the new media sometimes can be valuable in strengthening our relationships, we can never put this work on automatic pilot. What happens when we make a solemn agreement to put love first—before political convictions—even if ultimately we disagree? Differences do not necessarily dissolve. But such an agreement does help us to maintain a perspective that leads us to ask: how can I better understand the other? What can I do to heal a misunderstanding that may have crept into our discussion? How might the presence of love in our conversation illuminate the various angles of difficult questions, enriching us with perspectives that initially we may not have acknowledged? Practicing communication skills based on love and refining them can open us to wider perspectives and deeper insight into the issues themselves.

Real-Life Story
Working in Harmony[3]

I have been involved with town-level party politics for a number of years. At a certain point I served for two years as chair of the committee whose main job was to nominate and support the party's candidates for town board and other town positions.

When I joined the committee, I immediately noticed some difficulties in communication. For example, members would frequently force issues to the floor and push motions ahead before there had been sufficient time for discussion. This practice would often lead to arguments and harsh words, even to people walking out of meetings. When I became chair, I tried to facilitate a period of open discussion on issues before any motions were proposed, adding this period to the agenda for the meeting. This allowed everyone to be heard and to feel that they were part of the final decision when we chose to go to a motion at that particular meeting.

During my time as chair the entire town board, town justices, receiver of taxes, as well as both county legislature seats were up for re-election. We formed a candidate search committee, but it soon appeared that the committee was deeply divided, with very strong opinions in support of two different candidates for town supervisor. Before holding the actual meeting where a decision would be made, I decided to poll the group to determine whether we were split down the middle. This turned out to be a mistake, especially since I did not get a consensus on the wisdom of making this request. It led to outbursts, hurt feelings and personal resentments, including toward me.

The one who had initiated the argument later sent an email apologizing to the person he had offended, but he couldn't resist adding a few points of his own. What ensued was a series of ever more critical emails, with many others getting into the act. I realized that being "the first to love" meant trying to do something to stop the fight. I worried as I composed my email, because I had come to understand how much harm a hastily composed message could cause. I sensed that not everyone would be happy. But my request to lower the heat of the rhetoric and work together did put a stop to the email fight.

Hopeful, a few days later I called the vice-chair of the committee in order to discuss the next phase of our candidate search. To my astonishment, I found her very angry with me because she felt that I had forced her to make a public choice in front of others. I was hurt and overwhelmed, but I tried to restrain those feelings in order to listen as she shared her hurt. At the end we were able to salvage a sense of mutual respect, and even move to the constructive discussion of how to proceed with the work of the committee.

During that conversation I also learned that most members were confused about the process. To help clarify this, via email I communicated the plan that the vice-chair and I had developed together, including more interviews for the town board positions and proposed dates for the meeting to vote on our final recommendations to the main committee. When we did get together for the final meeting, it ran smoothly as if nothing had ever happened, as did the meeting of the whole committee when it made its final decisions. Relationships had been restored and we had found a new harmony in working together.

Step 3

Understand
Where There is Room
for Compromise
—and Not

*T*HE QUESTIONS THAT PROMPT the third step may be stated bluntly: "The practice of love is all fine and good, but what do we do given the fact that evil is at work in the world? Can we really close our eyes to the corrosive and manipulative effects of power, the loss of sacred values, and all of the ways in which human dignity is trampled? In these circumstances, might righteous anger be the best and fullest expression of love?"

The 2007 statement by the United States Conference of Catholic Bishops, *Forming Consciences for Faithful Citizenship*, explains: "There are some things we must never do, as individuals or as a society, because they are always incompatible with love of God and neighbor. Such actions are so deeply flawed that they are always opposed to the authentic good of persons. These are called 'intrinsically evil' actions. They must always be rejected and opposed and must never be condoned" (#22). In particular, "The direct and intentional destruction of innocent human life from the moment of conception until natural death is always wrong and is not just one issue among many. It must always be opposed" (#28).

But work in the political realm is not limited to identifying and avoiding evil. The bishops emphasize: "Opposition to intrinsically evil acts that undercut the dignity of the human person should also open our eyes to the good we must do, that is, to our positive duty to contribute to the common good and to act in solidarity with those in need" (#24). For example, the moral obligation to meet basic needs for food, shelter, health care, education, and meaningful work is also "universally binding on our consciences" (#25). The fact that the political choices about how to best meet these challenges are matters for principled debate "does not make them optional concerns or permit Catholics to dismiss or ignore Church teaching on these important issues" (#29).

Political life is not only a question of identifying what is good and what is bad. A large part of politics is discerning *how* as a community we will address what is bad, encourage what is good, and work together to make things better. For example, consider the problem of addiction to a drug such as heroin and its consequences in a given neighborhood community. It is definitely bad. But what should be done about it? Should our primary tool be the criminal law, with an emphasis on putting addicts in jail? This might help to make the streets safer for the community. Or would it be better to turn first to health policy, favoring treatment and rehabilitation over criminal sanctions? Or should we focus on the economic roots of the social problems that lead to drug use and addition? There are many different opinions and kinds of solutions. The fact that some people favor treatment over criminal sanctions does not mean that they take the problem lightly.

A Doctrinal Note from the Congregation for the Doctrine of the Faith, *Some Questions Regarding the Participation of Catholics in Public Life* (2002) distinguishes two kinds of pluralism. The first, "ethical pluralism," claims that citizens should have "complete autonomy with regard to their moral choices." In this view, every perspective is entitled to equal regard, and referring to moral anchors in political and policy discussion is considered imposition of the personal morality of some citizens on others. This kind of pluralism in the choice of moral principles or essential values poses a "real danger" to social life and the common good (#2).

The dangers of ethical pluralism should be distinguished from political pluralism: "the legitimate freedom of Catholic citizens to choose among the various political opinions that are compatible with faith and the natural moral law, and to select, according to their own criteria, what best corresponds to the needs of the common good" (#3). The Note explains: "On the level of concrete political action, there can generally be a plurality of political parties in which Catholics may exercise especially through legislative assemblies their right and duty to contribute to the public life of their country. This arises because of the contingent nature of certain choices regarding the ordering of society, the variety of strategies available for accomplishing or guaranteeing the same fundamental value, the possibility of different interpretations of the basic principles of political theory, and the technical complexity of many political problems" (#3).

Every issue— including bioethics— requires practical analysis about how society should deal with a particular evil. *Evangelium vitae*, John Paul II's letter on the Gospel of Life, which discusses abortion, euthanasia and the death penalty, points out that building a culture of life entails more than just naming the evil or removing "unjust laws."

> [I]t is not enough to remove unjust laws. The underlying causes of attacks on life have to be eliminated, especially by ensuring proper support for families and motherhood. A family policy must be the basis and driving force of all social policies. For this reason there need to be set in place social and political initiatives capable of guaranteeing conditions of true freedom of choice in matters of parenthood. It is also necessary to rethink labor, urban, residential and social service policies so as to harmonize working schedules with time available for the family, so that it becomes effectively possible to take care of children and the elderly. (#90)

Can clarity on principles be combined with open-minded discussion about how to make those principles a reality in our society? We should not be naïve about the scope and depth of the disagreements that permeate current discussions about law, politics and public policy. Nor should we rush into facile agreements. Nonetheless, I do believe that when I place myself before those who maintain a political perspective that is profoundly different from my own, I have much to gain from a sincere effort to listen and to understand the concerns and questions that may have shaped their perspective and approach.

For example, I can hold, as does Catholic teaching, that euthanasia is always wrong, with no room to waffle on that question. At the same time, in conversation with friends or colleagues who may disagree with this principle, I can also acknowledge that end-of-life care poses a set of difficult and painful questions, and it is not immediately clear how to establish the social structures that would insure the kind of care for the dying that would prevent anyone from being driven to the point of choosing euthanasia or assisted suicide. There are legitimate differences of opinion about how to address such policy concerns. We need the political process to work through what to do about this social problem, and how to insure that the ill and the dying are treated with dignity and respect. My friends and

I may have different ideas about how to vote on a proposition to legalize euthanasia, and if my friends are open to such exchange I will not hesitate to share with them the deep reasons for how I choose to vote. But even if we do not reach ultimate agreement, I can still recognize that I have much to learn from their observations, questions, and concerns about this issue.

Similarly, I can hold, as does Catholic teaching, that racism is always wrong. But at the same time, I can also acknowledge that the political strategies for addressing racism are not immediately clear, and that there are legitimate differences of opinion about what to do about it. I may find myself debating about education and labor policy—has race-based affirmative action run its course, or is it now more necessary than ever? We need the political process to work through what to do about racism in our society, how to reduce it, and how to build a culture in which every person is treated with dignity and respect. The fact that I recognize the need for that process takes nothing away from my commitment to the principle that racism is always wrong.

At what point do political conversations become intractable? At least some of the clashes come about because people may be speaking on two different levels: one side is clearly trying to identify the values at stake, while the other is struggling with the practical questions concerning how to resolve certain problems or address certain evils manifested in our social life.

The interplay between these two positions can be compared to a team of hikers in which one group is focused on the compass, which gives an accurate but fairly general sense of direction. Another is focused on a topographical map, and has carefully marked out the paths that have been closed due to rockslides or other obstacles. At times a certain layer of distrust sneaks into the conversation, which might take this form: "The topographical crowd does not want to forge across this rock pile because they really do not want to travel westward, and are trying to find every possible way to slow up our journey." Or, "The compass-obsessed want to force us across this rock pile because, in their heart of hearts, they really do not care about the weaker hikers and want to weed them out of our group."

What is the solution to this tension? Perhaps the heart of this step toward a positive vision of politics is believing that even when we disagree, the other's intention may be positive and constructive. It is a question of trust, of recognizing that we need each other, we need to open ourselves to the ways that the differences among us can help each of our perspectives to mature.

Real-Life Story
Across the Aisle[4]

Over the years, I have regularly attended Town Hall meetings with two well-known politicians from my neighborhood who are from a different political party than my own. Both of them are part of the party in power and have on various occasions voted to pass important and controversial legislation, some on topics that are very divisive.

These disagreements naturally made it a challenge to attend Town Hall meetings, especially since I was in the political minority. There were painful moments when I struggled with whether I should publicly express my opinion there. I decided to focus especially on building personal relationships with these officials, sensing that this might be more powerful than mere words. We often spoke after the meetings, they became acquainted with me, and when I would see them at other events they would greet me cordially.

One morning, I received a disturbing email from a friend. It was warning me that an issue which was important to me, and which the president had just put to rest with an executive order, was being put forward again at the state level under a different guise and that it would probably be passed. I was greatly bothered and saddened when I heard that the main proponent was one of my two friends. I felt betrayed and alienated.

I realized that I had to remain calm, get over my own feelings, and not take this personally. Further, I resolved to give this official the benefit of the doubt. People were emailing me to say that we should take action by protesting loudly and fighting back. I was not comfortable with this, especially since I had not yet had the chance to confirm that the information I had received was correct.

I decided to take the bull by the horns and to call her office — she was, after all, my representative. If she was indeed the author of the new bill, I preferred to hear it from her directly. When I called her office, I was told she was at the State House. I asked to speak to her assistant whom I knew and to whom I tried to be open and kind whenever I saw him. When he came to the phone he recognized my voice. I told him that I was concerned about the bill, and asked if his boss was indeed the author. He confirmed that she was, and also that she was aware that it was making many people angry.

I told him that although I respected his boss for the office that she held, as a citizen I disagreed strongly with the position she was taking on this issue. I expressed my concerns about how his bill would affect me if it passed and also noted that the president had gone in the opposite direction just the day before. We had a very cordial, open and constructive conversation.

After a few minutes he stopped and said to me: "You cannot imagine the barrage of insults, hate mail, and threats that this issue has caused over the past few days. You are the only person who has contacted us and who has been courteous, and I want to thank you. You don't know what this means to us, and by the way, the bill will not be put up for a vote. There is no chance of it passing. Thanks for calling and see you soon."

The next time I saw my representative, she asked me when I would come to the capitol and have lunch at the State House with her. Although we will always sit on "different sides of the aisle," we can still sit at the same table.

Real-Life Story
Handling Differences of Opinion[5]

As a photo enthusiast, I would often meet other photographers at opportune locations to capture nature's beauty. One of them I met often and we began to strike up conversations. Every so often he would express a political view that differed from mine. I would listen and could see how much he believed in what he expressed and how his personal story shaped his view.

Since we often exchanged emails sharing photos and good photo locations, he included me in his distribution list expressing his view on current political events. Presumably he thought that since our friendship was so congenial we must have similar opinions.

After several emails, I responded explaining my own view, which differed from his. While I expressed myself using no inflammatory language, I realized that doing so over the Internet was a gamble. I responded only to him so as to not embarrass him in front of others, which could have led to hostile exchanges rather than fruitful discussions. He responded in disagreement. We exchanged a few emails on the topic, agreed to disagree, and then continued to exchange emails on photography. Our friendship was strong enough to withstand the difference of opinion, and we continue to learn from each other.

A friend, who is also a fellow Christian, sends frequent emails about a particular social ideal with which I also agree. But there are other issues I believe in, most of which are not in line with his political perspective. After receiving one of his emails, I expressed a different opinion. After an email exchange, we agreed to speak on the phone. At first, we tried to convince the other of our own views, and I could feel the passion building inside. I wanted to show that I was right, but knew that I needed to hold back in order to listen. Even though we disagreed, I realized that I had learned a few things by listening to his perspective. Our views continue to differ and since we live far from each other, we do not see each other too often. When we did meet at an event, even though we were unable to talk at length, I could feel that there was an unspoken understanding that our relationship was intact. I look forward to continuing the discussion with him.

Step 4

Recognize
Suffering as a
Springboard for Love

*S*OME POLITICAL AND SOCIAL issues can tie us into knots because they hit so close to home and are so deeply bound up with personal experience. Amid heated discussion, at times it is helpful to stop and ask ourselves who is at the heart of these debates. Isn't it often a person or a group of people who in some way has been wounded? Do I think about the persons who are suffering because of these "issues" with the same love that I hope to have for a wounded Jesus on the cross? This fourth step asks us to pose this question: "Is my perspective on political issues grounded in an effort to love by entering into and living inside these wounds, and as much as possible, taking them on as my own?"

In *Forming Consciences*, the bishops note that identifying a particular action as intrinsically evil is the beginning, not the end, of a process that requires prudential reflection on the appropriate political response to a given evil. Continuing with the image of the hiking expedition, the concept of "intrinsic evil" resembles a guardrail. The guardrail does not preclude discussion about how to keep travelers from wandering too close to the edge. Nor does it preclude conversations about the effort that fellow travelers should, can, and will make to pull up those who may have fallen into a ravine. The guardrail itself is neither the path nor the goal of the journey.

Take, for example, a woman who may be struggling with how to deal with the financial, physical, and emotional demands of an unplanned pregnancy. Through the eyes of love, the woman facing these circumstances is a part of me, just as much as the child within her. Through this lens, one may share not only the joyful hope of a new life, but also the worries and uncertainties of those who feel pressured by economic burdens or social expectations, which can make it difficult to welcome the responsibility of a new child.

One person who lived this love in his life — seeing others as a part of himself, taking on their burdens, making room for their questions and problems, and pulling out from them all that is positive and building on that — was Jesus himself. The account of Jesus' conversation with the woman caught in the act of adultery (John 8:3-11 RSV) is a paradigmatic example. The scribes and the Pharisees brought the woman before Jesus and asked him, "Teacher, this woman has been caught in the act of adultery. Now in the law Moses commanded us to stone such. What do you say about her?" Jesus' oft-quoted response was: "Let him who is without sin among you be the first to throw a stone at her." When they heard this, one by one they went away, beginning with the eldest. Once Jesus was left alone with the woman he looked up and asked, "Woman, where are they? Has no one condemned you?" She responded, "No one, Lord." And Jesus said, "Neither do I condemn you; go and do not sin again."

Certainly Jesus did not equivocate on the content of the moral law, or on the fact that the woman's conduct was sinful — in fact, he concluded, "from now on do not sin anymore." But this was only after she had experienced his unconditional love: "Neither do I condemn you." In the television miniseries, *Jesus*, Mary Magdalene sums up the scene: "You treated her like she was worth something" (CBS 2000).

It was not so much the clarity of the law, nor its coercive force, but a personal encounter with the unconditional love of God that gave the woman the courage and strength to make a radical moral change in her life. Law is important — but, as John Paul II notes: "it is not enough to remove unjust laws." We also need to work on supporting the personal, cultural and social structures that can help to sustain people, especially those who are suffering, in their efforts to live a dignified human life.

By recognizing suffering as a springboard to love, we can hope to embody— individually and as a community — the living presence of Christ who brings to each person not only the clarity of moral truth, but also the personal courage to walk along his way and the consequent joy and beauty of his abundant and attractive life. For all who struggle deeply with the moral questions of our day, this living presence of Christ in the community can become a transformative encounter with the justice of Jesus, which is also love, mercy, and grace.

Real-Life Story
Agreeing to Disagree[6]

Dick: We have had a "mixed marriage" for more than fifty years. My wife, Shirley, is a Democrat, and I am a Republican. While other couples might have different opinions but do not care much for politics, both Shirley and I are highly committed and interested. We support different candidates and discuss the daily news at home.

Shirley: We met while attending college in Boston. Born in Massachusetts, I studied legal secretarial and accounting. It was always my dream to work in a law office; I wanted to work for social justice. Dick, who grew up in Maine, is a numbers guy; he studied accounting and retired as a buyer at IBM. As a young man he focused on the government's financial decisions. When we started dating, I assumed that he was a Democrat like me.

Dick: We agreed on the number of children we wanted to have, but we did not ask each other about our political opinions. When Shirley discovered that I was an active Republican, it was too late. We both understood that despite the differences we were meant for each other. Shirley supported me in my party-related work. But she did not change her opinion and her view of the world.

Shirley: As the years passed, our family grew. We were blessed with the nine children we wanted to have. Between raising them, working, moving from Maine to New York to Texas and eventually to Tucson, there was no time to get actively involved with politics. Discussions among us and with our friends, however, could heat up. I remember a time when we met with friends after church. Over coffee and donuts, some disrespectful remarks about government plans that I supported passionately led to an emotional outburst on my part. After that, we did not talk about politics anymore with these friends. But I felt bad and didn't have a solution.

The way through those difficult moments came not by chance but through little steps, daily acts of mutual understanding. We had embraced the gospel message and its call to mutual love, and we both felt attracted by this approach to integrate our faith into our everyday life. The gospel does not tell you which party you have to choose; you can be committed to one or the other, to emphasize good values and try to change others. There are many ways to serve others.

Dick: Reconciling these ideas started right at home. I understood that I had to be completely open to Shirley's ideas. And she in turn wanted to be empty and listen without prejudices. Together we learned how to handle teasing from friends. How could Shirley, a committed Catholic, vote for the Democrats?

Shirley: Being against abortion is only one aspect of how faith affects political decisions. A law does not resolve people's situations, either. After retiring, I became the Executive Director of the "Reach Out Pregnancy Center." One of many stories included a young woman who was determined to have an abortion because she feared her husband would leave her if she wouldn't. Mostly by my listening and being friendly and patient with her, she reached the decision to keep the baby. About three months later, she came back to our center and asked for maternity clothes. I was so happy to see her and asked how her husband was. She said he was very excited about the baby.

As director of a pregnancy center, I was required to attend quarterly board of director meetings. I was the only Democrat on the board. At one meeting, a board member became hostile toward me and asked how I could be pro-life and a Democrat. I was stunned and hurt by his very public remarks and surprised because we had a good working relationship. Whenever I needed something done, this member would be the one to step up and help out. I really wanted to lash out but I knew that the gospel called me to love this person. A couple of days later this member came into my office and apologized for his outburst.

Moving to Arizona, I found myself surrounded by a majority of friends who are Republicans. In 2008, I felt that I wanted to do more and work as a volunteer for the Obama campaign. Dick supported me immediately. Since we have only one car, it meant scheduling the car for my work at Democrat headquarters. And it meant that one day the Obama bumper sticker appeared, accompanied soon by the Romney edition. That was just the beginning. "Why do you have a bumper sticker for Obama on the right and one for Romney on the left side?" people would ask, "You can't decide?"

Often our friends asked how we could stay together without fighting. That was an opportunity to reveal our secret. Without living the gospel, I would not have made it. I remember how important it was for me to learn to put aside my thoughts in order to listen to others, to be open to others' views and to try to see the positive effort in the other party.

I do not agree with the whole Democratic program, and neither does Dick agree completely with the Republican.

Dick: We figured out some rules and rituals that work. Every evening we watch the news on CNN and on Fox. It helps us to see the issues from different perspectives. After that we always discuss the facts, without getting too emotional.

Indeed, the family atmosphere fostered a sense of citizenship. All of our nine children and twenty-two grandchildren are interested in politics, and some of them are active. How could it be any different?

Some are Republicans, and some are Democrats; family reunions are always marked by lively discussions. The relationship, though, is more important than any political issue.

I wouldn't change Shirley's political opinion, not a bit. She feels the same way about me. On the most important things in life, we agree.

Step 5
Build the *Polis* with Constructive Action

*L*ET'S RETURN TO THE question that opened this book: "So, what should we do?" When citizens sense that no political party matches their vision and hopes for human dignity and social life, what *can* we do? Feeling left out in the cold for too long, a kind of paralysis can set in. This step works to "defrost" three areas of citizen engagement with public life: voting, perspectives on public officials, and daily gestures of participation in public life.

Voting

A paralysis on voting is often rooted in a concern about crossing the line into what moral theology terms "cooperation with evil." In the past, some internet "voter guides" have described voting as a two-step process: first, identify "intrinsically evil" principles to which Catholic moral theology assigns only one acceptable position; second, vote for a candidate whose positions best match opposition to these evils. For many, this reasoning is attractive because it seems clear and easy to follow.

However, this two-step process falls short of the more complex reasoning in the U.S. Bishops' 2007 statement, *Forming Consciences for Faithful Citizenship*, which was re-proposed for the 2012 election. In that document, the bishops do not hedge on the question of "intrinsic evils," including abortion and euthanasia, which "... must always be rejected and opposed and must never be supported or condoned" (#22), as well as "human cloning and destructive research on human embryos....Other direct assaults on innocent human life and violations of human dignity, such as genocide, torture, racism, and the targeting of noncombatants in acts of terror or war, can never be justified" (#23). They also point out that some social issues are much more important than others: a well-formed conscience "recognizes that all issues do not carry the same moral weight and that the moral obligation to oppose intrinsically evil acts has a special claim on our consciences and our actions" (#37).

But *Forming Consciences* does not stop there. The task is not simply a matter of identifying principles, because a large role is given to prudence, the virtue that "shapes and informs our ability to deliberate over available alternatives, to determine what is most fitting to a specific context, and to act decisively" (#19). Decisions about voting entail a complex reflection, using "the framework of Catholic teaching to examine candidates' positions on issues affecting human life and dignity as well as issues of justice and peace" (#41). It also examines the candidates' "integrity, philosophy and performance" (#41) as well as their capacity to influence a given issue (#37).

Some voter guides have lifted out of context a statement from the 2002 *Doctrinal Note* (discussed above) which indicates that one is not permitted "to vote for a political program or an individual law that contradicts the fundamental contents of faith and morals" (#4). The *Note* was discussing the duties of elected officials, not voters. The bishops, in contrast, draw a clear distinction between these voting contexts. The voter's moral responsibility hinges on the voter's *intent*: "A Catholic cannot vote for a candidate who takes a position in favor of an intrinsic evil, such as abortion or racism, if the voter's intent is to support that position. In such cases a Catholic would be guilty of formal cooperation in grave evil" (#34).

On the other hand, the role of intent also means that "There may be times when a Catholic who rejects a candidate's unacceptable position may decide to vote for that candidate for other morally grave reasons. Voting in this way would be permissible only for truly grave moral reasons, not to advance narrow interests or partisan preferences or to ignore a fundamental moral evil" (#35). Further, the bishops warn that the intrinsic evil analysis should not become an excuse for a "single-issue" approach to voting: "[A] voter should not use a candidate's opposition to an intrinsic evil to justify indifference or inattentiveness to other important moral issues involving human life and dignity" (#34).

Thus the bishops' analysis in *Forming Consciences* would allow room for a number of complex considerations. For example, if one is considering the issue of abortion law and policy, questions could include:

- What institutional role does the position at stake play in shaping abortion law and policy? What will be the candidate's "capacity to influence" the issue?

- Regardless of the candidates' statement of principles, how effective will their specific social, economic, and legislative policies be in reducing the actual number of abortions in this country, and in the world?

- Given the special claim that the life issue holds, and given that the voter's intent is *not* to support pro-abortion policies, are there other "truly grave moral reasons" for rejecting or supporting a particular candidate? Considering the particular functions of the office at stake, where do the candidates stand and how will they implement other policies that foster or threaten human dignity and the protection of other — perhaps even numerous — innocent lives?

When a legislator raises a question about the content of laws and policies that deal with abortion, this person does not necessarily believe that abortion is a good thing. In *The Gospel of Life*, John Paul II acknowledges that current structures in the law may make it difficult to institute change. He writes: "[W]hen it is not possible to overturn or completely abrogate a pro-abortion law, an elected official, whose absolute personal opposition to procured abortion was well known, could licitly support proposals aimed at limiting the harm done by such a law and at lessening its negative consequences at the level of general opinion and public morality. This does not in fact represent an illicit cooperation with an unjust law, but rather a legitimate and proper attempt to limit its evil aspects" (#73).

According to *Forming Consciences*, the process of voting has more than two steps. Identifying "intrinsic evils" is extremely important, but it is not the end of the story. Just as a hiking expedition requires both a compass and a topographical map, a citizen's decision about which candidates to support should include not only identifying important values and principles, but also practical considerations about the candidate's capacities and qualities. Within Catholic traditions, civic engagement requires serious assessment of the gravity of the social issues and evils that plague our communities, and the firm intention to do what we can to protect human life and dignity wherever it is threatened. It also requires conscientious evaluation of the practical paths to reach those goals. Voting is not easy, but the task need not paralyze us.

Engaging Public Officials

Many in the United States sense that our political life has never been more polarized or frozen, especially concerning how we view our elected officials—especially those on "the other side." Is there any hope for a thaw in how we see and engage our elected officials?

Since 1996, the Focolare's Political Movement for Unity has been working to distill the principles of gospel-based love into a practical formula to be lived in the trenches of everyday political life. In several countries, politicians and public officials, often from different and even opposing parties, gather to encourage one another in their journey along this path. As Chiara Lubich explains in a 2003 address, this Movement is not a new party, "but the bearer of a new culture and new political practices." Key ideas include seeing the choice to become politically active as an act of love through which they respond to an authentic vocation, to a personal calling. "They want to provide an answer to a social need, to a problem in their city, to the sufferings of their people, to the needs of their times." Within this vision, they can see that others, even political opponents, might have made their choices out of love. Their stance is one of listening to everyone, including one's opponents. When there are conflicts, they try to "take the first step towards approaching the other person and reconnecting a breakdown in communication."[7]

At the National Parliament in Seoul, Korea, several legislators meet regularly to pursue similar goals. Representative Kim Nak-Sung reports that he keeps next to his telephone the points of "the art of loving in politics." He explains: "This way I remember to put them into practice in the course of my day-to-day work." Within this vision, public officials are engaged in what Chiara Lubich describes as the task of "political love": "to create and safeguard conditions which enable all other types of love to blossom: the love of young people who want to get married and who need a house and job; the love of those who want to study and who need schools and books; the love of those who have a business and who need roads and railways, clear and reliable rules."[8]

What would happen if we began to see our elected officials and candidates through these eyes? Might this hopeful, appreciative perspective help those in public life discern with more clarity their own vocation to serve, the vocation of others to service, and their deepest hopes for the community as a whole? When seen in this light, one can already feel the beginnings of a thaw.

Everyday Citizenship

Finally, expressions of citizenship are certainly not limited to voting on election day or specific interactions with public officials. Here are just a few ideas for constructive actions that can build the *polis* in daily life.

- **Be aware.** Make a conscious effort to seek out reliable information about local, national, and international issues. Find ways to learn about the particular problems and challenges that people are facing.

- **Be open.** Share your perspectives with local, regional, and national representatives. Give your input through town meetings, surveys, and other means of communication.

- **Be engaged.** Examine personal patterns of consumption, investment, and care for the natural environment. Volunteer time with local service organizations. Register to vote; vote in local elections; help others to vote. Support and participate in community events.

- **Be persistent.** Stay with situations until they are resolved. In situations of conflict, be open to the ideas of others and their different ways of solving problems.

- **Be an example.** Respecting laws that coordinate and ease the life of the social body — even ones that can be annoying, like traffic and parking regulations — demonstrates regard and love for fellow citizens and models citizenship for future generations.

Real-Life Story
Don't Forget the Golden Rule[9]

A short time ago I took the same oath of office that the President of the United States and all the members of Congress take. My position, however, is at the bottom rung of the political ladder. I was elected as an Advisory Neighborhood Commissioner in Washington, DC.

It all started when I moved into an apartment building in Washington. I noticed that as people used the elevator, passed in hallways, or met in laundry room, they did not acknowledge one another. As a Christian, I wanted to reach out. So I began my campaign: "Hi, I'm Mary, I live on the 7th floor." Many people responded; some did not. I resolved to respect each person's approach and continued with just a smile to those who did not respond. I noticed that some people began to greet each other; sometimes we would even hold open the elevator door to finish a thought. We were taking steps to become a community: individuals with different needs, of all ages, races, backgrounds, and levels of education.

Before long, we tenants ran into an obstacle with our landlord. The company managing the building asked us to enter into a "voluntary agreement," which seemed to promise stabilized rent if we could reach a 70% agreement among the tenants. Because the language was difficult, many of us signed only to discover later that we had lost our 24-hour front desk service! As individuals we would have had no legal basis to remedy this problem. So we formed a Tenant Association with the aim of getting back our front desk.

It was a long process, and among other things we came up against some attorneys who represented the largest landlords in the city. During the hearings I attended, I tried to listen to the attorney without prejudice, in order to understand better that landlord's side of the story. We did not win, but we had built a solid relationship as tenants with a common sense of purpose: to care for each other. With increased communication, we also became more aware of our neighbors' concrete needs, especially the elderly and those with limited financial resources.

Eventually 60% of the tenants joined the association, and I was elected chairperson. I understood my task as twofold. First, to respond as best I could to each person's concerns: from a perceived unfair rent increase, to a father just needing to talk about his child's problem, to dealing with management about issues concerning the building as a whole. Second, to increase our knowledge about the laws pertaining to tenants so that our lack of background in this area would not put us at a disadvantage.

Before long I was introduced to the office of the Chief Tenant Advocate for the District of Columbia and became a "stakeholder." We began working to reform outdated rental laws that were causing difficulties for many renters. I was chosen chairperson of the Rent Increase Group, which included both highly educated attorneys and folks who were ordinary but had valuable life experiences. As we began our work I encouraged the group to adopt a set of "ground rules": to offer and welcome every contribution as a good idea, aware that we would decide together on the best paths for reform. Over the course of our discussions we hit a few bumps in the road, causing hurt feelings. I tried to help each one to work through these challenges and return to the table to see each other with new eyes, as if we were meeting for the first time. When our working paper was presented to members of the DC City Council, we all felt that it expressed well our thought as a group.

A short time later I was asked to run to be the Advisory Neighborhood Commissioner for my district. I now represent about 2,000 of my immediate neighbors. I see this as an opportunity to keep the human person at the center of our community life, and in line with the Catholic Social Teaching principle of subsidiarity, to work toward resolving concrete problems on a level as close as possible to the affected persons. In every action we undertake, I try to be like the leaven that makes the bread rise. I continue to hold especially dear the last piece of advice given at the orientation for new Commissioners: "There are only two things to take away from today: be a good listener and don't forget the Golden Rule."

Resources

Documents:

Congregation for the Doctrine of the Faith, *Doctrinal Note on Some Questions Regarding the Participation of Catholics in Political Life* (November 21, 2002)

United States Conference of Catholic Bishops, *Forming Consciences for Faithful Citizenship* (2007 and 2012)

John Paul II, "The Vocation and the Mission of the Lay Faithful in the Church and in the World" (*Christifideles Laici*) (1988)

John Paul II, "The Gospel of Life," (*Evangelium Vitae*) (1995)

Applications and Examples:

Chiara Lubich, "The Charism of Unity and Politics," in *Essential Writings: Spirituality, Dialogue, Culture*, New City Press, 2007.

Mayor's Committee of Neighborhood Services, North Riverside, IL, "Neighbors All: Creating Community One Block at a Time," (2011) available at http://www.northriverside-il.org/file%20cabinet/recreation/neighborhood_services/NRNSManual.pdf

The Cube of Love, Teacher's Kit and Educational Guide, available at the Living City Magazine Website, http://www.livingcitymagazine.com/cube

Thomas Masters and Amy Uelmen, "A Common Commitment to the Common Good: A Spirituality of Unity and the Future of Public Life," Chapter 9 in *Focolare: Living a Spirituality of Unity in the United States*, New City Press (2011)

Articles:

Amelia J. Uelmen, " 'It's Hard Work': Reflections on Conscience and Citizenship in the Catholic Tradition," *Journal of Catholic Legal Studies* 47 (2008): 317-342.

Amelia J. Uelmen, "Reconciling Evangelization and Dialogue through Love of Neighbor," *Villanova Law Review* 52 (2007): 303-329.

Amelia J. Uelmen, "Traveling Light: *Pilgrim Law* and the Nexus between Law, Politics and Catholic Social Thought," *Journal of Law and Religion* 22 (2007): 445-479.

Amelia J. Uelmen, "The Spirituality of Communion: A Resource for Dialogue with Catholics in Public Life," *Catholic Lawyer* 43 (2004): 289-310.

Amy Uelmen, "Modern Means," *Living City* (June 2010).

Amy Uelmen, "A Positive Vision of Politics," *Living City* (August 2003).

Notes

1. Chiara Lubich, Innsbruck, Austria, November 9, 2001.
2. As shared by C.S.
3. As shared by P.D.
4. As shared by J.G.
5. As shared by Mike Murray.
6. As shared by D.M. and S.M.
7. Text available at http://www.centrochiaralubich.org/en/documents/videos/449-1000-cities-for-europe.html.
8. "Newsletter 01-05," http://mppu.org/downloads/cat_view/91-newsletter.html, Author's translation.
9. As shared by Mary C. Young.

New City Press
of the Focolare
Hyde Park, New York

New City Press is one of more than 20 publishing houses sponsored by the Focolare, a movement founded by Chiara Lubich to help bring about the realization of Jesus' prayer: "That all may be one" (John 17:21). In view of that goal, New City Press publishes books and resources that enrich the lives of people and help all to strive toward the unity of the entire human family. We are a member of the Association of Catholic Publishers.

Other Books in the 5 Step Series
www.NewCityPress.com

5 Steps to Effective Student Leadership	978-1-56548-509-9	$4.95
5 Steps to Living Christian Unity	978-1-56548-501-3	$4.95
5 Steps to Facing Suffering	978-1-56548-502-0	$4.95

Scan to join our mailing list for discounts and promotions

Periodicals
Living City Magazine, www.livingcitymagazine.com
(See November 2013 issue dedicated
to getting involved in the community.)